Communication

Enhance Your Interpersonal Communication Proficiency, Mitigate Uncomfortable Dialogues, And Exert Indirect Influence On Individuals

(Enhancing Communication Skills Via The Practice Of Imitation)

Leigh James

TABLE OF CONTENT

Barriers To Effective Communication 1

Ensuring Audibility And Comprehensibility In Communication 7

Persuasive Discourse In The Era Of Digitalization 24

An Appeal To Foster Empathy: A Pivotal Component Of Flourishing Interpersonal Bonds And Effective Dialogue 52

How To Effectively Convey Your Message Through Written Communication – While Maintaining Reader Interest 110

The Study Of Interpersonal Dynamics With The Aim Of Addressing Challenges Encountered In Developing Social Relationships 134

Failure To Adequately Study Will Result In Your Inability To Successfully Navigate Or Fulfill The Requirements Of This Academic Endeavor .. 149

A Self-Reflection On Being Assertive 158

Barriers To Effective Communication

If you have engaged in perusing this literary piece, it is highly likely that you possess the perception that your aptitude in the domain of communication necessitates improvement. While an immediate remedy for communication issues may not exist, identifying potential barriers that impede effective communication is a commendable initial stride towards enhancing one's communication aptitude. A number of prevalent factors that impede efficient communication include:

Fear of Being Judged

One factor contributing to individuals' difficulty in effectively conveying their thoughts and ideas to others is a apprehension of instant evaluation. Despite possessing significant ideas, individuals afflicted with this particular fear often exhibit a tendency to withdraw and abstain from expressing their thoughts. To become a competent communicator, it is crucial to eliminate this initial barrier.

Stereotyping

Prior encounters have the capacity to influence our methods of communication and interpersonal connections. Individuals who have encountered unfavorable circumstances in the past may develop preconceived notions towards others, perceiving them as potential risks, and restrict their interactions solely to their familiar social circle. To eradicate this practice, it necessitates maintaining a receptive attitude and expanding one's outlook.

Speaking a Different "Language"

One of the most conspicuous impediments to effective communication lies in conversing in a language distinct from that of the recipient. However, linguistic disparity encompasses more than just engaging in varied dialects. It additionally entails the utilization of unfamiliar terminology or complex vocabulary, both of which can have a detrimental effect on effective communication.

Given that the utilization of a divergent linguistic medium poses a significant obstacle to effective communication, it is imperative to possess a thorough understanding of one's audience. Make an effort to acquaint yourself with your audience prior to speaking, in order to effectively address them using a language that they are acquainted with.

Indecision

If an individual is faced with challenges in decision-making or struggles with the organization of their thoughts, it is essential to address indecision as a communication obstacle in need of improvement.

Uncertainty can pose as an impediment to effective communication across various aspects of life, extending from delivering presentations in client gatherings to expressing the need for a salary increment. Precision is of utmost significance in order to effectively convey your message to your audience, and to achieve precision, assertiveness is required.

Overwhelming Yourself with Emotion

Experiencing a sense of apprehension prior to delivering a significant public address is a commonly shared occurrence among orators. However, when this apprehension transforms into an overwhelming state that cannot be effectively controlled, the impact of your message is diminished. The aforementioned holds true when your discourse or the conveyed information elicits excessive anger, joy, fear, or distress within you. In the event of your incapacity to manage these emotions, notwithstanding the perception of your audience regarding your fervor and authenticity in delivering your message, it greatly hampers the reception thereof.

Insufficient Knowledge

Establishing a meaningful connection with individuals can prove challenging if one lacks familiarity with the subject matter being deliberated. In the event that you encounter a subject with which you are unfamiliar, it is advisable to inquire and pose queries that will aid in your comprehension of the matter.

If you find yourself in the position of receiving such a communication, expressing opinions or offering feedback on a subject where your expertise is lacking rather than robust can potentially generate bewilderment or misinterpretation between yourself and the recipient of your response. Rather than offering your personal viewpoint, it would be prudent to inquire further regarding the subject matter in order to enhance your comprehension of the topic at hand.

Information Overload

Frequently, individuals tend to erect a barrier or disengage when they perceive an excessive amount of information being conveyed, rendering the act of extensively expounding on a subject solely to awe one's audience with knowledge largely ineffective. Rather, endeavor to be explicit and succinct.

Now that you have concluded perusing this chapter, we invite you to reflect upon your own behavior and discern whether any of the aforementioned negative communication practices manifest in your own conduct. If you perceive that you are culpable of any of these behaviors, eradicate them promptly.

Ensuring Audibility And Comprehensibility In Communication

Skilled presenters effectively exhibit qualities of resilience, assurance, soundness, expertise, autonomy, poise, and ease in their interactions with both the audience and the environment. Nonverbal communication is of utmost importance. During this expedition, we shall explore the crucial aspects to prioritize in order to ensure that your physical demeanor conveys the intended message accurately.

When addressing a public gathering, it is essential to acknowledge that individuals in the audience harbor desires and aspirations as they assume their positions, along with certain anticipations while attentively hearing your discourse. It is imperative to demonstrate reverence towards these aspirations and anticipations in order to deliver a compelling presentation. The audience anticipates that you will meet these expectations. At the commencement of each presentation, there lies the expectation that you will accomplish precisely that. However, when this requirement is not fulfilled, it is possible that your audience may experience a decline in their confidence in you. They grow disillusioned as their needs and desires remain unfulfilled.

A successful presentation encompasses more than just creating a favorable impact. You must first establish the foundation. With this underlying basis, you are now equipped to ensure that your message is received with a receptive demeanor. After successfully capturing the interest of your audience, now is the opportune moment for you to issue a call to action. In order to prompt your audience to undertake said action, it is imperative to effectively sway, exert influence upon, and convincingly persuade them.

Appearance

What is the initial observation that we make regarding a speaker? It's the speaker's appearance. What apparel is the speaker adorned in? What is the person's grooming like? The mere presence of the speaker effectively communicates a message to the audience. Does the speaker possess intellect, systematic qualities, a sense of organization, or a level of self-assurance? All of these cues are being conveyed prior to the opportunity for verbal expression. The manner in which you carry yourself is already conveying a message to the audience. It is crucial to bear in mind that you are delivering a presentation, wherein a substantial component lies in the nonverbal signals you convey to your audience. We all want to send out the right kind of message.

Proper packaging holds significant importance in the sale of books, as initial impressions carry substantial weight. It is equally crucial when endeavoring to promote oneself, disseminate relevant information, and effectively convey one's message to the intended audience. The audience you are addressing is attempting to arrive at a similar decision as a discerning consumer evaluating a book within a bookstore. Does the information hold significance in relation to my personal circumstances? Does it hold sufficient value for me to allocate my time and resources towards paying attention? Will I truly derive any advantages from the information you are about to share? Many of those initial decisions will be based on the perception of you even before you speak. In the pursuit of establishing a positive initial impression with your audience, where do you commence your endeavors? What strategies can you employ in order to establish your credibility and promptly grab the attention of your audience, thereby presenting yourself in a favorable manner? You guessed it. It commences with your attire and personal appearance.

Being aptly suited not only provides an affirmative validation of your credibility to your audience, but also instills a sense of self-assurance within you. There appears to be a divergence in our behavior when we are attired in more formal attire. We are inclined to exhibit a higher level of refinement and decorum when attired in formal attire such as a coat and tie or a dress. It elicits a positive sensation within us. And such positive emotions are immediately transmitted to your presentation when you gaze upon your audience.

Posture

An unmistakable indication of an ineffective speaker is the display of inadequate posture while addressing the audience from the podium. In the context of public speaking, it is essential for the speaker to consistently consider their positioning in relation to the audience. Following the audience's assessment of your attire, the subsequent focal point of their attention lies on your posture at the lectern. The way you position yourself at the podium or lectern conveys various signals to your audience. The manner in which you position yourself during your presentation will convey valuable insights into your attitude towards the content, self-perception, and above all, your regard for the audience.

Maintaining proper posture during your presentation is essential.

While proper respiration and articulate speech are commendable, an exemplary public speaker typically complements their proficient vocal abilities with a posture that exudes strength and confidence.

In contemporary society, individuals are prone to passing overly critical judgments based on physical appearance, and in formal settings, it is commonplace for us to hastily form opinions about someone based on their demeanor or body language.

Consider individuals who are adept at public speaking, such as former educators, professional associates, sales professionals, or political figures, and observe their posture while delivering a speech.

Fundamentally, achieving an impressive posture entails elevating the chest and lowering the back. The exercises provided in this section are intended to assist in achieving the aforementioned goal by realigning the spine and stimulating the chest.

What are the characteristics of proper speaking posture? In my opinion, a proper posture while speaking should be established prior to entering the speaking area. As a presenter, it is essential that you approach the lectern with a sense of assuredness. It is advisable that you refrain from keeping your head down or your hands held behind your back. It is recommended that you present yourself to the audience by maintaining a stance where your feet are positioned slightly apart, your shoulders are held upright, and your back is maintained in a straight posture. I understand that my words may give the impression of summoning you, akin to the manner in which individuals are called to attention within the military. Well, you are right. That's the idea. This approach will promptly capture the interest of your audience, prompting them to adopt a more attentive posture and redirect their gaze towards you. Additionally, it will indicate to your body and mind that you are ready to engage in verbal communication. You are prepared to embark upon the challenge that awaits within the arena. You possess the necessary readiness, assurance, and composure to confront and confront them. Having proper posture can yield all of these benefits for you.

Having correct posture will immediately establish a strong rapport between you and your audience. They will perceive that you are adequately equipped and fully prepared to convey the message. Your elevated shoulders will result in your gaze being directed straight ahead towards your audience. You will have the opportunity to witness their countenances as they likewise observe yours. This will provide you with your initial immersive interaction with your audience. This modest demeanor will swiftly establish a connection, along with an impression that you possess authority and deserve their attentive ear.

Is it advisable for you to maintain this stance throughout the entirety of your presentation? Negative. This serves as your initial maneuver. It is similar to assuming the initial positions in a game of football. Prior to the initiation of the play, all players assume their respective predetermined positions. The position conveys that all participants are prepared to commence. After the commencement of the ball's release, all participants promptly engage in designated activities. Your speech is equivalent in nature. After delivering your initial remarks, carefully crafted to seize the interest of your audience, it is now appropriate to transition to the subsequent stage of your presentation, involving bodily movements. Please bear in mind that this is merely your initial positioning for the game. Subsequently, employ your physicality to narrate the tale.

Many speakers position themselves behind the podium. In certain scenarios, it is considered the most preferable course of action when delivering your presentation. The arrangement of the room may necessitate that this particular spot be utilized as the sole location from which you may address the audience. However, if it is feasible for you to relocate, I recommend stepping away from the lectern and actively involving your audience.

Stepping away from the lectern during the presentation will imbue a sense of forward motion. It is possible to involve your entire physique in the delivery of the presentation. Stepping away from the podium provides you with the chance to establish a connection with the audience. You are able to maneuver among them and establish a close proximity. Do not confine yourself to a singular section of the stage. Navigate across the stage and actively interact with various sections of the venue. Ensure that you have your notes in your possession.

The Tarot card drawn is the Seven of Pentacles.

The Seven of Pentacles can also be viewed favorably, albeit contingent upon one's willingness to exercise patience. If one draws the Seven of Pentacles, it suggests that the progression of their relationship will not occur swiftly.

You are in the presence of a twin flame who desires to engage in activities that align with their objectives

Adhere to the appropriate procedure and proceed at a leisurely pace. Although this is not incorrect, it may be necessary to occasionally guide them towards the appropriate path.

The protracted duration of waiting associated with the Seven of Pentacles necessitates a deliberation on whether one wishes to continue awaiting a desired outcome. If, for any conceivable reason, there exists a temporal constraint on the various significant achievements you aspire to share with your ideal partner, it is indicative that this person may not align with your long-term objectives.

If you possess an inclination to ascertain the emotions of your twin flame, it can be inferred from the Seven of Pentacles

that the sentiments held by your counterpart will progressively amplify and assume a more amorous nature as time elapses. Whilst the prospect appears optimistic, nothing can be assured, necessitating the consideration of whether you are prepared to endure the wait for reciprocation of affection.
16

EMPRESS TAROT CARD

Does obtaining the Empress card in a love reading indicate good fortune? Affirmative, as the Empress embodies the essence of love. She epitomizes affection and caregiving. She exhibits attributes of kindness, empathy, and maturity.

The Empress emanates a deep sense of love that instills unwavering trust in the face of adversity, assuring that all will be well. It is through the Empress's nurturing love that one discovers the strength to overcome past wounds and restore one's inner self.

The Empress personifies love, indicating that she embodies it

Achievement lies in the power of love, as it ultimately serves as the greatest triumph.

If one establishes a connection with the Empress, individuals will be drawn towards their persona akin to a moth's instinctive attraction towards illumination. Individuals are notably enamored by your company, and you may discern that their experiences are enriched by your mere presence, surpassing any benefits that you personally derive from being in their company. Your penchant for optimism and unwavering positivity renders you an exceptional individual to associate with, as your presence invariably uplifts those fortunate enough to spend time in your company, leaving them with a heightened sense of self-worth and a more optimistic outlook on existence overall. The higher self of your twin flame is deeply astounded by your remarkable capacity to restore the well-being of others and the remarkable growth of your intuitive capabilities. You exhibit steadfastness and dependability in matters of affection.

Your present disposition demonstrates a composed attitude in matters of love, and you exhibit no signs of desperation or urgency. You hold a firm belief in the power of love and possess unwavering confidence in its enduring strength. Your doppelgänger is exceedingly fortunate to possess your presence.

In regards to your twin flame, the Empress signifies an individual who will provide such profound love that your existence will be encompassed by a deep sense of abundance.

Persuasive Discourse In The Era Of Digitalization

In our rapidly evolving and digitally interconnected society, it is often overlooked that face-to-face interaction holds immense potency and significance. However, as individuals who have engaged in sincere and substantive dialogues can attest, there exists a distinct and profound quality in the act of making eye contact and openly expressing one's sentiments and ideas. When executed skillfully, writing possesses an immensely influential capacity to forge connections with individuals. The majority of individuals do not compose articulate texts or email correspondence, nonetheless, this hurried replacement for substantial interaction can be intricate.
Texting

It has achieved widespread prevalence as a prominent means of communication. Although text messaging can serve as an effective means of maintaining communication with loved ones, it can also inadvertently give rise to misinterpretations and hostilities. In order to ensure that your textual communications effectively convey the intended message, it is crucial to carefully contemplate both the substance and manner in which they are presented. The subsequent information consists of a set of recommendations for proficiently communicating through text messages:

When considering the substance of your writing, strive for clarity and brevity. The addressee should possess the ability to comprehend your intended message without the necessity of conjecture or interpretation. Refrain from employing abbreviations or informal language when interacting with individuals who possess limited knowledge of such terms.

It is equally essential to take into consideration the overall tone employed in your text. The intended tone is frequently conveyed through the employment of emojis and vivid language rather than the specific choice of words. For instance, if you intend to convey a sense of playfulness or amiability, you may employ a greater number of emojis and exclamation points within your textual communication. The strategic use of an appropriately chosen emoji or amusing GIF has the ability to imbue your textual communications with a touch of individuality and bring about a sense of lightness, particularly in situations where you perceive it to be necessary.

Please bear in mind that texts are frequently interpreted without the benefit of context; as such, it is crucial to exercise caution in selecting your words. If there is uncertainty regarding how the recipient will perceive the content of your message, it is advisable to exercise prudence and choose the more cautious approach. Be direct. If the communication seems excessively straightforward or impersonal, incorporating a gif or emoji can bring some additional flair. Consider the possibility of the recipient misinterpreting your message, and therefore, strive for brevity. Taking these guidelines into consideration, texting can serve as an excellent means of maintaining connectivity.

Texting and Online Dating

In text-based communication, the absence of facial expressions and body language deprives one of visual cues to discern the thoughts or emotions of the other party. In situations where individuals have yet to establish a physical acquaintance, there exists a lack of prior information to guide our deductions. Consequently, our interpretations of written communication rely heavily on our imaginative faculties. Hence, it is crucial to be mindful of the vocabulary and demeanor employed in your communications. Exercise extreme caution in regards to potential misunderstandings and extend the other individual the presumption of good intentions.

Texting can help you get a better sense of someone's personality and how they communicate. Additionally, it can serve as an enjoyable means of engaging in playful banter, fostering connection, and ensuring a smooth and continuous exchange of dialogue. Utilizing optimistic and cheerful words will facilitate the establishment of a robust rapport with your counterpart. In the event that you require assistance in initiating a conversation, consider employing open-ended queries that will elicit a more extensive disclosure from your corresponding individual.

Although direct interpersonal communication is considered optimal, circumstances may arise where such interaction is not feasible. This mode of communication is founded on the concept that language can be employed to elicit profound emotional responses in individuals. To put it differently, the selection of our words can exert an influence on an individual's perception of us.

Employ these three techniques to enhance the persuasiveness of your written communications:

1. Convey optimistic messages: Make sure your messages exhibit a positive and uplifting tone. The avoidance of

negativity is recommended, as it may potentially elicit a negative response from the other party. If you possess a penchant for sarcastic humor, it would be advisable to reserve it for in-person interactions. The use of sarcastic remarks often fails to convey its intended meaning accurately in written form, particularly in situations where there is a lack of familiarity between individuals.

2. Employ powerful language: Exercise caution in your word selection, opting for language that is potent and evocative. Language possesses considerable influence; hence, exercise judiciousness in its employment. Prioritize careful consideration when communicating through text, especially when a message might be susceptible to ambivalence – ensure utmost clarity in your choice of words.

3. Employ a proactive approach: Refrain from utilizing passive language or expressions such as 'I think' or 'maybe we could.' Instead, opt for active phrases such as 'I am enthusiastic about visiting that exhibit, would you be interested in accompanying me?' or 'What do you say we give that new restaurant a try?' The manner of expression employed here effectively communicates engagement and determination.

Texting and Romantic Relationships

In contemporary times, it is observed that romantic partners are almost equally inclined to engage in communication via electronic devices as they are to engage in face-to-face interactions. Although the use of text messaging can offer convenience in maintaining communication, it can also give rise to novel difficulties.

Couples may engage in heated discussions or prolong tense

conversations initiated in person through the use of text communication. Given the susceptibility of texts to misinterpretation, they possess the capacity to precipitate volatile misapprehensions. Furthermore, couples may observe that the act of texting hampers their capacity to engage in efficient and meaningful communication. When endeavoring to convey intricate emotions or subjects via written correspondence, there is a propensity for the intended meaning to become obscured in the process of interpretation. Engaging in an argument that originated from an in-person interaction through text messaging can result in detrimental consequences and is advisable to steer clear of.

There are innumerable emotional facets associated with conflict resolution that cannot be adequately expressed via a text message. If an individual is inclined towards engaging in heated exchanges via text messages with anyone, it is worth reflecting upon the number of disagreements that have been successfully resolved through this medium. Any? Alternatively, does engaging in a textual exchange merely serve to extend the discussion until an insurmountable barrier is encountered and the issue is subsequently resolved during a subsequent discourse?

Notwithstanding the difficulties that may arise in the context of romantic relationships, it is worth noting that there are also certain advantages associated with texting. Text messaging offers a commendable means of maintaining regular communication with one's significant other throughout the course of the day. Furthermore, it can serve as a convenient method of communication in situations where verbal conversation or face-to-face interactions are not feasible. Furthermore, when employed judiciously, the act of sending text messages can cultivate a sense of closeness and foster a deeper bond within a romantic affiliation.

There exist, however, certain deviations from the norm. Certain individuals may perceive text-based communication as a more preferable mode of interaction due to its characteristic of allowing for thoughtful deliberation, free from interruptions. This facilitates the opportunity for more contemplative and profound discussions. In essence, the impact of texting on romantic relationships is contingent upon its utilization. When employed with careful deliberation and regard for the desires of one's partner, texting can prove to be a formidable instrument for fostering closeness and establishing a bond.

Chapter 7: Encouraging Verbose Communication

We have all encountered dialogues that come to a standstill. You have exhausted all topics of discussion. The dialogue has reached an impasse. There exist numerous strategies to sustain the ongoing dialogue. Chapter 4 presents a viable approach to addressing this matter. Through the practice of attentive listening, one can pose inquiries that encourage further discussion. Additional alternatives encompass providing succinct replies.

Demonstrating prompt responsiveness indicates your engagement in the discourse, as well as a desire to sustain its flow without undue verbosity. Currently, it is imperative to confirm that the brief replies exhibit a positive nature. Please demonstrate an elevated level of vocal emphasis when providing a concise response.

Additionally, kindly exhibit a smile while providing your response. The act of promptly providing responses can be likened to expressing an implicit encouragement to continue, urging further elaboration or requesting the continuation of the dialogue, all without explicitly uttering those phrases. This approach will minimize idle periods and foster continuous engagement with the interlocutor.

This strategy is particularly advantageous for individuals who display reticence and prefer not to engage in extensive verbal communication. You have the option to offer brief responses by demonstrating sincere attentiveness while allowing someone else to monopolize the conversation. When engaging in conversation with someone and lacking knowledge about the topic they are discussing, I resort to employing this approach. There is no justification for feigning comprehension of their words; rather, I display genuine interest and afford them the opportunity to express their knowledge to its fullest extent. Certainly, should the individual inquire about my familiarity with the subject matter, I shall forthrightly disclose the truth.

There are potential drawbacks associated with engaging in this activity, particularly if one begins to do so without conscious awareness. I have encountered instances where individuals have engaged in prolonged conversations with me despite providing brief replies. Now, I have acquired the knowledge on how to gracefully disengage from such conversations, particularly those in which I lack any interest. Chapter 11 will provide comprehensive coverage on the topic of concluding conversations. However, it is important to note that there may be certain disadvantages associated with this approach, particularly when engaging in such conversations with individuals who possess a propensity for extensive dialogue.

It is recommended that your responses be concise and limited to a single word. Apply the necessary emphasis to that particular word. For instance, one could express surprise by exclaiming "oh my!" or displaying curiosity through phrases like "indeed?" or "is that so?" Conveying understanding can be achieved by nodding in agreement, employing an inquisitive intonation, and affirming with "alright." Demonstrating consensus with someone's viewpoint can be achieved by nodding and replying with "indeed." Remember, simplicity is crucial in this matter. To successfully execute this strategy, all one must focus on is the proper tonal nuances and selecting a single word for emphasis.

Below are a few illustrations showcasing how this phenomenon manifests itself across various conversational contexts. I am effectively conveying the tone and significance associated with the word by placing it in parentheses.

Example #1 Friend's House:

Acquaintance: I visited Home Depot recently.

Me: "Very well" (Inquisitive, I am eager to hear additional details.)

Eample #2 At Work

I find it advantageous to opine that our new supervisor exhibits a pronounced tendency towards micromanagement, dear colleague.

Me: Yeah. (Extremely obvious, I agree.)

Example #3 Close Acquaintance Sharing Favorable News:

Acquaintance: I have reached a definitive conclusion to pursue a career in nursing and have duly submitted my application for admission, with the intention of commencing my studies in the forthcoming months.

It gives me immense pleasure to express my excitement and extend heartfelt congratulations to you for your remarkable achievement. I feel a great sense of pride for your accomplishment.

Acquaintance: It is quite astonishing the level of affordability that the nursing program offers. I am pursuing this opportunity via the local community college, with a tuition fee of merely $7500.

Me: Really? (To my astonishment, I am utterly taken aback by the remarkably affordable cost of nursing school.)

Companion: Oh indeed, it is quite remarkable that this long-awaited event has come to fruition. I was informed by my mother in the past that I did not possess the intellectual capability required to pursue a career in nursing.

Me: Seriously? (Presenting a serious demeanor, it appears that your mother lacks knowledge on the subject.)

Friend: Indeed, I shall prove it to her. They have informed us that it is permissible for us to conduct guided tours of the campus for our acquaintances and relatives prior to commencing our activities. I had anticipated that you would be interested in accompanying me to witness it.

Me: Absolutely.

As evident from the observations, this concept can be effortlessly executed. There is an infinite range of potential responses. Through the application of this technique, you can engage in extensive conversations with minimal exertion on your behalf. This statement aligns with the assertions made in previous chapters regarding the innate human inclination towards seeking attention and validation through active listening. Concisely responding to others provides individuals with an opportunity to express their thoughts, fosters the development of a solid connection, and demands minimal exertion on your behalf.

Exercise #7.1

There exist a couple of approaches to enhance this particular skill, namely through collaborative efforts with a partner or by engaging in routine conversations. If you desire to engage in collaborative practice, we recommend sitting down and kindly requesting your partner to initiate a conversation. They have the ability to engage in discussions pertaining to a wide range of topics, be it a subject of their preference, a narrative, or any matter that they can sustain lengthy discourse on. During instances when they encounter a deceleration or break in the narrative, provide a fitting monosyllabic reaction. Ensure that you employ the appropriate emphasis and tonal quality. Instruct your partner to cease if the word disrupts the cohesion of the text. Now, provided that the word and accent align appropriately, the partner should proceed with the ongoing discourse.

Applying this method in casual discussions functions similarly to the exercise. Endeavor to provide concise responses periodically throughout the day. If you identify a suitable moment to employ them during a conversation, endeavor to do so. This can be carried out in the company of colleagues, acquaintances, relatives, and so forth. Any individual that you come across presents an opportunity to hone this particular skill. Just as has been the case consistently, the greater frequency with which you engage in this activity will lead to its gradual integration into your conversational repertoire. I anticipate our reunion in the upcoming chapter.

Nevertheless, it is crucial to consistently strive for the most salubrious approach to maintaining relationships with your loved ones, especially when making an ongoing effort to empathize, comprehend, and embrace their perspectives on the world. Furthermore, it sometimes involves the task of expressing challenging remarks or potentially disrupting the relevant relationship.

A Word About Leadership
Two crucial instances from my personal encounters: "Trust" and "Being in a position of advantage."

To begin with, it is imperative to acknowledge that compelling individuals to visit undesired destinations is an infeasible task. Consequently, it becomes crucial to ascertain their current location and skillfully lead them towards a designated destination, which may diverge from their initial preferences. In order to guide individuals through unfamiliar, unfamiliar, or potentially unsettling environments, it is vital to establish a sense of trust. Consequently, it becomes imperative to adjust and align oneself with their particular circumstances and surroundings. In order to guide individuals towards a particular destination, it is imperative to possess a comprehensive understanding of the landscape to which you aspire to lead them, and personally acquaint yourself with that unexplored domain. In order for any progress to be made, it is crucial for them to place their trust in your expertise and comprehension before considering any other factors.

They must also hold the conviction that you harbor genuine concern for their well-being at a level equal to their own, that you share a profound connection with them, and that your bond transcends any ulterior motives or concealed intentions.

Effective leadership necessitates the cultivation of trust, a task that can be greatly facilitated by an in-depth understanding of the thoughts, emotions, and situations of those individuals with whom one collaborates.

As a leader, the significance of attributing and accommodating is more essential than ever before, as it is the relational equity developed over time that determines the true value of what you possess.

Furthermore, undertaking the responsibility of guiding individuals inherently suggests that you are, in essence, "leading," being ahead of them due to your prior exposure and examination of the subject matter to a certain degree. Exercise prudence, as there will be no discernible form to trail should one venture too far in advance.

Despite your extensive travels, they would merely have the capability to handle the initial endeavor in that direction. In the event of initiating a significant lead, individuals may not only manifest reluctance to conform to your lead, but also possibly fail to acknowledge your presence altogether.

The fundamental significance of creativity lies in empathy, wherein one possesses the aptitude to amalgamate their perspective with the current reality of others. As individuals in positions of leadership, we often exemplify a spirit of innovation, surpass conventional boundaries, and explore novel territories.

Upon my revelation, it has come to my attention that whenever I experience empathy, I am invariably struck by the ponderous question of, "What was the genesis of this profound sentiment within me?" What was my experience like when embarking on this initial course of action? Subsequently, I will adapt my speech to incorporate this newfound understanding.

You might already possess the advantage as you hold the requisite authority to do so. You may have a significant advantage over others." "You may possess a considerable lead compared to others." "You may be significantly more advanced than others." "You may enjoy a substantial head start over others." "You may have a noteworthy edge compared to others. However, upholding a slight advantage may require demonstrating empathy towards your community.

It may be necessary for you to make a temporary return.

As the person responsible for overseeing a particular matter, it is of paramount importance to consistently maintain an understanding of the perspectives, emotions, and encounters of those who encompass your customer base, stakeholders, and associates.

Conclusion: A Closing Remark

In the event that you possess exceptional material, it is possible that it may not resonate with all individuals should you fail to demonstrate empathy towards your audience or exhibit disregard towards them.

There is a possibility that there will be no one observing you.

Always speak with empathy.

Take into account the perspective of the other party and make necessary adjustments to every aspect of your communication.

Your proficiency in communicating will be enhanced.

An Appeal To Foster Empathy: A Pivotal Component Of Flourishing Interpersonal Bonds And Effective Dialogue

Empathy serves as the cornerstone for cultivating constructive and reliable connections.

In the latest electoral processes for the United States presidency and the Brexit referendum, a conspicuous absence of compassion was observed on the global platform. The leaders of political parties and pollsters exhibited a lack of understanding towards the electorate. Policymakers devoted a significant amount of time to scrutinizing each other rather than engaging in meaningful dialogue. Citizens, lacking sincere effort to understand others, have chosen sides and crafted oversimplified portrayals of them.

Furthermore, beyond the realm of politics, a heightened sense of empathy is indispensable in various spheres such as communities, families, and business enterprises, as well as all other aspects of human existence.

Empathy is the skill of communication, relationship-building, and conflict resolution that remains severely underutilized and underdeveloped. Nevertheless, it is both essential and influential. If establishing prosperous connections is deemed vital to achieve success in both personal and professional spheres, then demonstrating empathy emerges as the cornerstone of fostering successful interpersonal relationships.

The accord lacks compassionate understanding.

Empathy refers to the ability to understand, empathize with, and place oneself in the circumstances of another individual, thereby thinking and feeling in alignment with their experiences. It does not indicate a complete understanding on your part. It is not obligatory for you to agree. When one demonstrates empathy, he or she actively seeks to understand and foster a sense of being understood in another individual.

Although empathy is not a complex notion, it is not an arduous concept.

What factors contribute to the difficulty and scarcity associated with locating this item?

It poses a threat. I might discover that my unwavering position is limited or unveiled when I sincerely attempt to comprehend an individual's perspective. I may potentially be compelled to adapt my cognitive framework.

It has feelings. Occasionally, an adverse perception can evoke a considerably greater sense of fear compared to an unwelcome perspective. I can empathize with the potential sense of peculiarity and discomfort that one might experience were they to find themselves in a similar circumstance. I had the opportunity to empathize with the emotions of the other individual. I have no inclination to make an effort in understanding my intense emotions during such moments. My body undergoes a physiological shift into a state of self-preservation, which further complicates the development of social skills.

It is demeaning. If my capacity for empathy is genuine, I might also come to realize that the other individual does not possess the level of insanity, foolishness, incorrectness, or cruelty as I had previously assumed. This would function as a gentle reminder to myself of my limited knowledge and understanding. Should I engage in derogatory remarks to bolster my own position, I would be willing to humbly lower myself a few notches.

Methods to Enhance or Elevate Your Empathy Quotient

While it is more expedient to instill empathy in individuals when they are young, it is still possible for adults to acquire and enhance their empathetic capacities. The subsequent methods can be employed to augment empathy.

Read Books Of Fiction

In opposition to prevailing viewpoints, engaging with works of fiction has the potential to enhance levels of empathy. Based on recent research findings, individuals experience a distinct cognitive sensation of immersing themselves in an alternate realm when engaging with works of fiction.

This discovery holds great importance as it serves to illustrate how individuals have the capacity to establish an authentic connection with those who exist beyond their immediate sphere. This serves as evidence that individuals are capable of establishing meaningful connections with individuals whose lifestyles significantly diverge from their own, when considering a realistic scenario. Individuals hailing from the United States, for instance, may peruse a literary work depicting the life of an individual residing in China, thereby acquiring the ability to establish a connection with someone situated at a great geographic distance.

A recent study revealed that, as opposed to the commonly held external viewpoint, the act of reading fiction enables us to grasp characters' behaviors through immersing ourselves in their circumstances and thoughts, thus adopting their internal perspectives. Put simply, literature grants us the opportunity to understand the thoughts and perspectives of individuals in circumstances that would typically remain inaccessible to us.

Listen

An exceptionally effective means of fostering empathy is through actively listening to others. Understanding the thoughts and emotions of others becomes attainable when we make a conscientious effort to lend an ear to their perspectives.

The most exceptional form of attentive listening arises when we set aside our preconceptions and personal viewpoints, directing our undivided attention towards comprehending the words and ideas expressed by another individual. By eliminating potential diversions such as mobile phones and tablets, we can enhance our listening capabilities to a greater extent.

If we dedicate our complete attention to others, they will experience a sense of being nurtured and understood, granting us the opportunity to truly grasp their perspective.

Make an effort to comprehend individuals who possess divergent viewpoints and convictions.

Numerous individuals perceive it as considerably easier to establish a connection with individuals who belong to our "in-group." Put differently, it is notably simpler to place trust in or establish a rapport with those whom we perceive to be akin to us. In a heterogeneous professional setting, such a mindset may impose limitations or impede the authentic comprehension of individuals who lie beyond our communal boundaries.

It is imperative to allocate sufficient time for understanding individuals who possess diverse perspectives, thereby prompting reconsideration of our own thought processes. In order to enhance empathy, individuals may have to address their own biases and preconceived notions, while considering the perspective of others.

Individuals can additionally engage in this behavior by expanding their social networks and cultivating relationships with individuals whom they do not typically associate with. It is conceivable that they might experience astonishment upon discovering that their similarities surpass their initial perceptions, and it is even likelier that they will cultivate heightened empathy as a consequence.

Effectively conveying empathy necessitates effort and acquiring valuable life experiences.

Many individuals require constant reinforcement of Captain Obvious' counsel on demonstrating empathy:

Engage in active listening and refrain from excessive speaking. Make an effort to actively listen for 70% of the duration of any conversation, particularly if you tend to dominate the discussion. Please come prepared with relevant inquiries instead of making comments during the discussion.

Connect to hear. While the act of actively seeking information and attempting to solve issues through listening may be preferable to a complete absence of listening, it does not always lead to the cultivation of relationships based on trust. An effective and intelligent approach to dialogue entails actively engaging in empathetic listening.

Allow the other individual to assume control. Permit the other person to assume a leadership role. Facilitate the other person in taking charge. Enable the other individual to take the initiative. Maintaining a firm standpoint exacerbates the complexity of the matter. Nonetheless, you will achieve greater success in articulating your perspective with empathy during your turn if you have initially made a sincere effort to actively listen and empathize with the other party by placing yourself in their shoes or considering their position.

Prior to proceeding further, ensure that you acknowledge individuals' comprehension. Cultivate the practice of reiterating their words, providing a rephrased version, or employing an alternate method to confirm your comprehension before proceeding with your own explanation or before they proceed to address the next concern. Despite the potential to impede progress, this precautionary measure could ultimately result in time savings should the situation escalate to excessively high temperatures.

There are numerous opportunities to engage in the practice of empathy. Merely a cursory look at the news, the individual nearby, or the individual residing across the corridor would suffice. May I inquire as to the location of your upcoming opportunity to display compassion?

Not Moving From Unproductive Topics

Have you ever encountered situations where you endeavored to engage someone in a discussion regarding a particular matter, only to observe their lack of interest or enthusiasm, resulting in terse and uninterested responses? In the event that this occurrence takes place, it is imperative that you transition the discussion to a different subject and proceed accordingly. It is imperative to engage in strategic subject transitions in order to uphold the flow and productivity of a conversation. Should the individual display a lack of interest in engaging in the conversation, it is prudent to acknowledge that the current subject matter is not resonating with them. In addition, there will be instances in which the discourse fails to progress. An often encountered rationale behind this error is the desire to cultivate or sustain an engaging conversation. Additionally, this could be attributed to their presumed adherence to a prearranged script that guides their thoughts and speech. Regrettably, it is beyond your jurisdiction to regulate discourse and determine the topics of conversation for others. Nevertheless, should you desire to engage in a discussion, you may certainly make use of a compilation of subjects for consultation. It is important to refrain from exerting pressure in any conversation.

Similarly, it is crucial to bear in mind that engaging in discussions of unsuitable subject matters should be avoided. It is advisable to refrain from discussing offensive, excessively personal, or controversial subjects unless it is certain that the individual you are communicating with does not mind. Regardless of whether you are jesting or engaged in a sincere conversation, it is of no consequence. One prevalent cause of the widespread failure to comprehend this or commit this error is the tendency to overlook the fact that the entirety of the world population does not share the same perspective or level of understanding. For example, certain individuals within your family or even a collective of friends may find themselves at ease with discussing a particular subject, whereas the rest feel less inclined to do so.

Not Listening Well

The act of attentive listening seems to have diminished in contemporary society. If one is disinclined to lend an ear, meaningful dialogue is bound to devolve into a mere cacophony of voices. Have you ever attempted to convey or discuss a matter, only to perceive a lack of receptiveness from those around you? Did you feel discouraged? Did this conduct result in you forming the belief that the information you were sharing held no value to others' time or attention? How did you feel? It is likely that you experienced negative emotions such as distress, incomprehension, and a sense of being disregarded. It is inadvisable to engage in such behavior towards others. It is of utmost importance that you actively listen when someone else is speaking. If your attention is diverted, you display disinterest in the discussion, or your nonverbal cues convey the same sentiment, it is probable that individuals will discontinue engagement with you in conversation.

In the event of a deficiency in your listening skills, there is a higher likelihood of encountering issues such as interrupting others and committing the conversational errors outlined within this section. Failure to actively listen will result in a lack of awareness regarding the perspectives and information being conveyed by others. As a result, you will potentially fail to retain pertinent information that was communicated to you during the course of the conversation. Insufficient listening abilities or a lack of capacity to attentively listen to others can also give the impression of being excessively self-centered. All aforementioned portrayals effectively terminate the dialogue. It will diminish others' inclination to engage in conversation with you.

Constantly Correcting Others

There exists inherent uniqueness among individuals, resulting in a multitude of distinctions between us. Additionally, there are variations in our methods or manner of communication. It is imperative to refrain from engaging in the continual or unnecessary correction of others during conversations as it may be considered a common error in discourse. It can be quite vexing when someone attempts to correct you, particularly regarding trivial matters. Should these specific particulars prove to be unrelated to the central argument they are expressing, the situation is exacerbated to a greater degree. It not only disrupts the overall discourse but also has the potential to instill feelings of inferiority in others. Please bear in mind that when you choose to address someone's trivial error, you are essentially highlighting their mistake and drawing unnecessary attention to them in an unfavorable manner. The choice of one's tone can elicit various impressions, potentially giving rise to perceptions of being pedantic, snobbish, or even condescending. Given that these qualities are all unfavorable attributes to be linked with, it is imperative to be mindful of your communication with others. Certain individuals prioritize logic, accuracy, and other traits to a greater extent than others. If you perceive that this statement is relevant to your situation, it is likely that you experience a sense of annoyance when someone utters something that is factually inaccurate. Have you ever experienced the inclination to rectify the statements of others, and sensed an internal unrest when you refrain from doing so? It is imperative to initiate a transformation given the current circumstances.

Prior to succumbing to the inclination of correcting individuals, it is advisable to reflect upon the potential benefits that may be derived from such an action. Consider whether you are causing more detrimental effects than beneficial outcomes. Additionally, it is essential to contemplate whether the information you are disseminating is of interest or relevance to others. Do you perceive the statements made by others as inaccurate or inappropriate in relation to your personal principles and convictions? Through deliberate contemplation of these inquiries, one can mitigate the inclination to rectify the actions of one's peers.

Children

Interacting with children markedly differs from other modes of communication. When engaging in conversations with children, it is common to aim at instructing them or imparting valuable lessons. You are not opening something up for discussion or trying to get feedback. You are endeavoring to foster comprehension and elicit proactive response from them.

Word Choice

It may be highly enticing to employ contemporary colloquial expressions when interacting with children in an effort to establish rapport. This has the potential to be a grave error. If the usage of colloquial language is erroneous, the intended message becomes obscured. Furthermore, irrespective of one's proficiency in employing colloquial language with accuracy, the child might derive entertainment from the utilization of such slang terms, thereby detracting their attention from the intended underlying message.

Additionally, it is crucial to consistently consider the child's age during your interactions. It is advisable to refrain from employing complex vocabulary when communicating with young children. Ensure that you are employing a lexicon that is acquainted to them. Assisting a child in expanding their vocabulary holds significance; nevertheless, it is not opportune to undertake this endeavor during a crucial deliberation or instructional juncture.

The majority of parents possess knowledge regarding the linguistic proficiency of their children. In the event that you are uncertain about their comprehension of a particular word to adequately grasp your message, it is most prudent to abstain from employing it within the context of the conversation. You have the option to return to the topic and educate them on the word at a later point in time.

Tone

When engaging in conversations with children, it is advisable to assume a demeanor characterized by firmness and assertiveness. You aim to facilitate the bestowal of respect upon yourself, while reciprocally demonstrating respect towards them. Instead of using a curious and candid intonation as one would employ when speaking to a partner or parent, it is preferable to adopt a tone that conveys authority.

Exercise caution in maintaining a moderate tone while communicating with children. Numerous youngsters exhibit a tendency to disregard or ignore adults when they resort to raising their vocal intensity. Additionally, it is common for children to associate a raised voice with feelings of anger or disappointment. If the aim is not to discipline the child, this approach may prove to be counterproductive.

Body Language

Children possess a comparatively limited capacity to interpret and understand non-verbal cues, hence the significance attributed to body language in interactions with adults is not equally applicable in conversations with children. However, it can be helpful to take up a closed stance. Assuming a defensive posture by intersecting your arms across your chest or firmly placing your hands on your lap can effectively transmit to the child the gravity of the situation, making it clear that it is not up for debate.

Active Listening

Active listening is crucial in facilitating effective communication with children, albeit in a uniquely distinct manner. Juveniles have not yet acquired independent active listening abilities. It is crucial to ensure that they comprehend the information you are conveying to them. Kindly request the child to articulate the information you have conveyed using their own choice of words, if feasible. This will ensure that they are actively listening to you and you can clarify if there are any misunderstandings.

Example Conversation

In this illustrative dialogue, a paternal figure is elucidating to his juvenile offspring the reasons behind refraining from engaging in bullying behavior towards other children at the designated bus stop. Whilst discipline is indeed a component of the dialogue, the primary objective is to impart a valuable educational experience. Observe the manner in which the various attributes of effective communication are being employed.

Father: My comprehension entails that you partook in the act of intimidating fellow individuals at the bus stop earlier today. Would you be inclined to provide me with information regarding the matter at hand? The father carefully selects his words to provide the child with clarity regarding the nature of the conversation and affords him an opportunity to articulate his perspective.

Son: Yeah, so what? Recently, I have noticed a tendency for them to exclude me, consequently leading to my retaliatory actions. They deserved it.

Father: I see. Thus, it seemed to you that you were being subjected to unwarranted targeting, and accordingly responded to such perceived treatment? Active listening.

Son: Indeed, I suppose that would be accurate.

Father: It is imperative for you to comprehend that resorting to intimidation towards other children, regardless of the emotional distress they may have caused you, is unacceptable. There exist alternative approaches to address those emotions. On future occasions, it would be advisable to kindly request their inclusion in their recreational activities. Their response may elicit surprise.

Son: Really? I believe they would simply disregard my presence or mock me in response.

Father: What would be the consequence in the event that they were to do so? It is unnecessary to associate with acquaintances who derive amusement at your expense. In the event of such occurrence, you may opt to avert your attention and engage in independent activities while awaiting the arrival of the bus. You are prohibited from causing harm to other children. Kindly inform me of your intended course of action in the event that you are excluded from their theatrical production tomorrow. Evaluating the child's level of attentive engagement.

Son: I intend to inquire whether they would permit me to join their activity, and should they decline or respond with amusement, I will proceed to engage in the solitary activity of reading a comic book beneath the tree until the arrival of the bus.

Father: Thank you. That concept has considerable merit. The tone is firm yet composed and courteous.

During the course of this conversation, it is possible that the father will assume a standing position while the child remains seated, in order to convey a serious and weighty tone to the situation. This non-verbal communication conveys the message that this gathering is intended to be more instructional in nature, rather than a mere dialogue, with the purpose of penalizing the misconduct of bullying towards other children.

Shrinking newsrooms

Internationally, as a result of the impact caused by the digital transformation of all industries, including the media sector, news organizations are experiencing a reduction in staff size, as the number of employed journalists continues to decrease on a daily basis.

What is the significance of this concept to professionals in the field of public relations? There are those who assert that it will have negligible impact on our approach to conducting business.

However, considering that media relations is at the heart of our public relations work, the dynamics in the new environment will undoubtedly be markedly dissimilar.

Provided that we are able to establish strategic alliances with media entities for the purpose of crafting and presenting narratives, the significance of a PR professional's role will persist, irrespective of external alterations.

Indeed, given the prevailing circumstances where the newsroom faces significant demands to increase productivity while operating with limited resources, it is opportune for any public relations practitioner to assume the role of a collaborator in the media industry.

The essential question is this: to what extent are we, as PR professionals, capable of generating content that is easily shared, easily digested, and laser-focused on the needs and interests of customers? Such content should have the potential to catch the attention of newsrooms, who can then validate and distribute it to their readership.

Are we concerned about maintaining the integrity of the information so that we may meet the qualifications of being trusted content partners?

There may exist a series of inquiries similar to this, which, if we are able to respond affirmatively to, will establish us as reliable collaborators for the diminishing journalistic sphere.

Considering this viewpoint, the downsizing of news organizations presents a significant potential for public relations firms and professionals.

Collaborate or perish

Although this statement may sound trite, we are currently living in an era characterized by continuous news coverage, with newsrooms around the world working tirelessly to deliver what they consider to be crucial news updates to the public.

However, it should be noted that in our current era, the media is facing heightened scrutiny from its audience. Social media, for better or worse, has played a significant role in this phenomenon, allowing consumers to be more vigilant and critical of the media's efforts. Additionally, critics who possess a thorough understanding of social media have become more adept at challenging any misrepresentation or factual errors that may accompany the rapid dissemination of news and opinions.

In the current era of social 3.0, characterized by the rapid shaping of news and perspectives, how can one effectively fulfill the role of a more proficient public relations practitioner?

The public relations professional caters to his clientele, providing them with strategically curated information to be disseminated effectively within the desired media channels including both traditional and social platforms. The purpose of his proficiency in the field of communication is to cater to the requirements of the client who acts as a consumer.

Conversely, the public relations professional also caters to the requirements of journalists. A proficient and knowledgeable public relations professional possesses the ability to effectively provide journalists with accurate and pertinent information. Additionally, they can effectively convey forthcoming industry trends in products, services, or innovations, and fortify the knowledge and understanding of their clients in the media.

The role of the PR profession has undergone a profound transformation. Instead of solely disseminating press releases or focusing on organizing press conferences, PR professionals and agencies now actively engage in co-creation and collaboration with their clients, as well as with the journalistic community.

There is a considerable level of rivalry for attracting attention and securing considerable viewership/ readership, even for every concise unit of information such as 140 characters, that are enriched with newsworthy updates and have the potential to influence what gets amplified in the media.

For the conscientious journalists and media organizations, who aspire to establish themselves as reputable providers of up-to-date information and influential opinions, it is imperative to seek individuals who can foster collaboration and participate in the joint creation of content.

The responsibility to assume this role rests with public relations professionals who aspire to significantly impact their clients. A crucial inquiry that every public relations professional or agency should pose to themselves on a daily basis is whether they actively participate in collaboration and co-creation processes.

This recipe will have a profound impact, both presently and in the long term.

PR is content engine.

It has been observed multiple times within this literature that various businesses are experiencing a significant shift, attributable to the emergence of innovative methodologies, advancements in technology, and the diminishing boundaries of both geography and the workplace. In light of this overarching trend, it is evident that the realm of public relations, as both a trade and a practice, is similarly subject to these transformative forces.

Examine the narrative of any literature discussing contemporary patterns, and one can observe a substantial body of work elucidating the potential decline in significance of public relations experts. This can be attributed to the escalating direct involvement of media in corporate outreach endeavors.

Does this imply that the viability of the PR professional will face progressively greater hardships?

Yes, to an extent. However, if the public relations professional possesses a comprehensive understanding of current trends and perceives the necessity to adapt their practices accordingly, the prospect of facing obsolescence becomes highly unlikely.

As previously mentioned, contemporary public relations no longer revolves solely around the creation of press releases and their indiscriminate distribution to the media in hopes of obtaining coverage. This constitutes merely a fraction of the broader scope in which PR can operate.

The downsizing of newsrooms, although regrettable, can provide unexpected advantages for PR professionals who possess the acumen to identify opportunities and offer valuable expertise. This implies that the journalist is currently engaged in his editorial pursuits, facing stricter time constraints, and allocating lesser time for activities such as extensive research and analysis.

Proficient public relations professionals have evolved their roles beyond mere reputation management, expanding their expertise to encompass content creation for their clients.

The consumption of high-quality content plays a paramount role in achieving visibility in the field of business. The sole means by which a client's narrative can achieve superior communication, thereby distinguishing itself amidst a sea of comparable entities, involves the creation of narratives that are distinct and groundbreaking. In order to achieve this, public relations professionals must engage in an iterative process of determining the most effective narrative projection, ensuring that it captivates the audience and effectively disseminating it to the media, with the aim of generating even a modicum of enthusiasm towards the company.

Journalists, when provided with information, are equally eager to gain a comprehensive understanding of the industry's dynamics, the company's position within the market, the competitors present, and their unique selling propositions (USPs). Exclusively through this comprehensive approach will they attain a comprehensive perspective of the pitch, thereby empowering them to determine its newsworthiness.

Frequently, in the contemporary landscape, where the media is experiencing pressure from various sources, there is rarely enough time available for them to conduct in-depth investigations, even if they assume that the subject matter is intriguing.

The precise juncture at which public relations must function as content generation engines arises, whereby all available information, including industry data, client and competitor details, and unique selling points (USPs), must be disseminated and shared.

If this information can be instantly accessible to the media, it significantly facilitates their endeavors and facilitates the pursuit of their story pitch.

This example serves as evidence that serving as a creator of content can significantly contribute to the effectiveness of the PR pitch, bringing satisfaction to both the PR agency and the client whose reputation is being managed.

In this manner, there exist a plethora of ways in which serving as a content generator will prove advantageous to the public relations industry, thereby providing added value to both clients and media outlets.

Potential Impact on Individuals

Certainly, the inclination to prioritize others' satisfaction is not entirely detrimental. In the context of a romantic partnership, it is essential to consider and prioritize the emotions, necessities, and desires of the other individual involved. Such inclinations typically stem from a deep sense of fondness and solicitude.

Nevertheless, prioritizing the satisfaction of others at the expense of one's own emotions and desires could potentially have detrimental effects on both personal well-being and interpersonal bonds.

"Presented below are a series of consequences that arise from the act of striving to satisfy the expectations of others:

You experience feelings of resentment and frustration.

If one consistently engages in acts of assistance, the recipients of such aid may, to some extent, acknowledge and perceive these selfless efforts. However, it is not an absolute certainty that they shall do so. Over a duration of time, individuals may progressively exploit your goodwill, even if their underlying purpose isn't to do so. They may be unaware of the sacrifices you have been making on their behalf.

Regardless of the circumstances, exhibiting kindness while harboring hidden agendas can result in feelings of resentment and frustration. This has the potential to manifest as passive-aggressive behaviors that may cause distress or bewilderment among individuals who are unaware of the underlying situation.

Others Take Advantage

Some people may recognize and take advantage of your people-pleasing efforts. They may find difficulty in ascribing a label to their conduct, but due to their awareness of your willingness to comply with their requests, they persist in making further demands. You will persist in affirming due to your desire for their satisfaction.

This could potentially entail significant repercussions. The presence of family and friends who consistently request financial assistance may lead to significant financial difficulties. There is a possibility that you could be more susceptible to experiencing emotional or psychological mistreatment and manipulation.

If an individual has offspring, being excessively preoccupied with pleasing others may yield additional ramifications. It is permissible to exempt your child from performing their assigned tasks with the intention of fostering affection and esteem between the two of you. This hinders their acquisition of essential life skills. Presently, they may be experiencing contentment, however, it will not be long before they encounter arduous lessons that pertain to the concept of accountability.

Relationships Aren't Satisfying

Robust and sound relationships are characterized by equilibrium and reciprocity among the parties involved.

You do things for the ones you love, and they should do the same in return. You will not be able to establish meaningful relationships when individuals in your circle solely appreciate you based on the tasks you perform for them.

Authentic concern for others cannot be treated as a commodity. If one perceives oneself as someone who consistently engages in altruistic acts, yet experiences resentment and a sense of being undervalued, it is indicative of a lack of genuine self-connection. It can be challenging to uphold gratifying relationships without genuinely being attentive to oneself.

Experiencing Exhaustion and Overwhelm

The most significant consequence of seeking approval from others is a perpetual state of stress. This may occur when one assumes responsibilities beyond their capabilities. Not only are you foregoing the valuable personal time you require, but you also lack the necessary time to fulfill your obligations. In order to achieve the desired outcomes, it is necessary to labor late into the evening, frequently depriving oneself of sufficient rest. This will inevitably result in physiological ramifications, along with psychological distress including heightened levels of anxiety and concern.

The individuals in your vicinity experience feelings of frustration.

Your partner may take notice of your tendency to consistently concur with others and question why you consistently apologize for actions for which you bear no responsibility. One can easily fall into the practice of consistently offering assistance to those who are not intimately connected, while neglecting to invest effort and time in their personal relationships.

Furthermore, succumbing to the tendency of being excessively accommodating may prove detrimental if one consistently engages in actions for the sake of satisfying others, to the extent that their self-sufficiency becomes compromised. It is imperative to bear in mind that individuals in your immediate vicinity may exhibit strong displeasure if you fail to uphold honesty, or if you inaccurately alter the factual details of events solely to protect their emotions.

You display a lack of trust

Individuals who exhibit people-pleasing tendencies frequently refrain from complete honesty in their interactions with others, as their behaviors are primarily driven by the desire to fulfill their people-pleasing inclinations. When you're aware that you're capable of lying convincingly, it won't be long until you start mistrusting others. There will consistently remain a sense of skepticism within your thoughts regarding the veracity of their genuineness.

Nonverbal Communication of Men

The prevalence of male body language is not universal across all males. In any event, there are certain aspects of nonverbal communication that commonly occur among a substantial number of men. Male body language is frequently perceived to be more assertive and commanding in nature. Women are occasionally encouraged to adapt their male counterparts' body language in the professional setting.

Placement: Males frequently choose expansive stances in order to enhance their physique. Maintaining an open stance with legs slightly apart and an upright posture, whether sitting or standing, signifies confidence; on the contrary, displaying closed body language does not convey the same sense of assurance.

Eye contact: While it is common for men to establish visual contact, prolonged eye contact can be perceived as overwhelming or intimidating. Occasional displays of ocular aversion are commonplace. Similar to women, understudies expand their horizons through curiosity.

In contemplation: It is not customary for men to engage in introspection regarding one another. They frequently showcase women in order to demonstrate their superiority.

Lower limbs: Similar to women, a man's legs and feet typically serve to enhance his appearance. This incorporates sentimental premium.

Smiling: It is observed that men display smiles less frequently than women in social environments; they tend to be more reserved in their outward expressions. They do, however, occasionally employ forced smiles. Men frequently display a smile when in a positive mood or in an effort to gain an advantage over others.

Regarding physical discomfort, men tend to experience greater unease compared to women. This is not truly suggestive of weakness or fatigue, but rather a strategy to harness energy.

The non-verbal communication exhibited by females, or women, bears notable resemblance to that of males.

DISPARITIES IN FEMININE NONVERBAL CUES

1. WOMEN'S COQUETTISH CONDUCT

Individuals exhibit significantly diverse approaches towards romantic relationships. Presented below are some of the subtle and deliberate behaviors that women employ in order to allure and captivate a man:

Similar to Marilyn Monroe, when women attempt to seduce a man, it often leads to an uproar and an exhibition of allure, reminiscent of the expression women display when they experience pleasure.

An alternative way to say the same thing in a formal tone could be: "Redirecting one's gaze in an upward and sideward direction towards a gentleman can be interpreted as an additional inviting gesture from a lady towards a man."

An oblique glance accompanied by an elevated shoulder highlights the curvature and contours of the feminine visage. This denotes the presence of estrogen, exposes the vulnerability of the neck, and emits pheromones. Women instinctively engage in this behavior as a means of enticing others.

The size of a woman's external genitalia is commensurate with the size of her labia. This phenomenon is referred to as self-mimicry, which attracts male individuals. Women accentuate their lips by applying glossy or vibrant-colored lipstick.

Women sometimes playfully flip their hair or touch their necks to attract attention, as this reveals the armpit area that emits pheromones, emphasizes the graceful curve of the neck, and showcases glossy and luxurious strands of hair.

Women who possess large eyes, a petite nose, well-defined lips, and prominent cheekbones tend to be regarded as more captivating by men. This preference is rooted in the association of these features with higher levels of estrogen, signifying greater affluence in women. In the male demographic, women tend to appreciate well-developed leg, buttock, chest, and arm muscles. The posterior region of a gentleman tends to be highly favored among females as their primary choice of male physical feature.

2. The Contrast Between Decisiveness and Submissiveness.

Women struggle to strike a balance between being assertive and not intimidating men. From the perspective of nonverbal communication, this phenomenon manifests in diverse ways. Women employ signals of "adaptation" to express vulnerability, and moreover, they can employ specific strategies to demonstrate confidence and establish that they are not easily deceived.

Women tend to shape their eyebrows higher on the brow as it creates a perception of increased vulnerability. This phenomenon triggers a release of hormones within the male psyche that is closely tied to the instinctual drive to protect and safeguard the female individual.

Curiously, a relaxed or exposed wrist can be interpreted as a sign of readiness to adapt, and it is typically observed among women and homosexual men who subconsciously employ this gesture to attract individuals in social settings. This is why many women, while smoking, choose to hold the cigarette with an exposed, textured wrist.

When women desire to exude confidence, they can maintain a wider stance with their feet positioned more distantly apart. This act of "guaranteeing an area" serves as an internal indicator for men that the woman is experiencing a sense of confidence.

3. Women and Deception

People lie differently. Their motivations for deceit vary:

Males engage in deceit in order to present themselves as more exceptional, captivating, and successful. They frequently misrepresent themselves to a greater degree than they do others.

Women tend to exhibit greater honesty in regards to self-representation, prioritizing the protection of others' emotions or boosting their self-esteem through strategic social interactions.

4. WOMEN AND NONVERBAL COMMUNICATION SIGNALS

Women excel in decoding and interpreting nonverbal cues more proficiently than their male counterparts. Allow me to disclose the confidential information:

Monica Moore, an esteemed researcher of Experimental Psychology at Webster University in St. Louis, has made the significant finding that men frequently fail to perceive the initial visual attraction cues exhibited by women. Typically, women are required to establish repeated eye contact in order to capture the attention of a man.

In a separate inquiry, individuals were approached to decipher a mute motion picture. Females possessed the opportunity to contemplate the situation approximately 87 percent of the time, while males displayed an accurate understanding merely 42 percent of the time. Curiously, individuals who identify as gay and men in occupations that require exceptional levels of emotional engagement, such as nursing, education, and acting, displayed similar patterns of behavior to that of women.

Females might exhibit a heightened ability in discerning nonverbal cues due to their increased cognitive engagement when evaluating the conduct of individuals. X-ray filters reveal that women possess 14 to 16 active regions in their minds while evaluating others, whereas men only have four to six active regions.

5. ADVICE FOR BOTH MALES AND FEMALES

Taking into consideration a selection of nonverbal cues exhibited by females, the following suggestions are provided for the benefit of both parties involved:

When initiating interaction with a woman, it is advisable for men to avoid approaching her from behind, as this may lead to her feeling apprehensive. They find themselves in a highly advantageous position by gaining entry at a single juncture and subsequently maintaining a single point of presence.

It is unnecessary for one to possess perfect expectations in order to attract a gentleman. Research indicates that men are gravitated towards women who engage in flirtatious behavior as a means of indicating their availability, as opposed to being drawn to the most physically attractive woman present.

How To Effectively Convey Your Message Through Written Communication – While Maintaining Reader Interest

I find composing in the academic style to be unappealing due to its monotonous nature, frequent regression to the introductory points, prolonged path to the intended destination, and subsequent loss of supporting details along the way.

However, it holds a distinct position within academia. If your intention is to engage with individuals outside the scientific community, specifically the broader public, it is important to adopt the role of a communicator rather than a scientist or a member of the general public. Please note that I acknowledge scientists are indeed real people. In a subsequent section, I will delve into the examination of role theory in relation to the portrayal of scientists, however, for brevity, let me summarize by stating that a role refers to the contextual framework in a given circumstance, with the specific context in this instance being science, while the circumstance pertains to the act of communication.

I urge you to approach your writing not from a scientific perspective, but from a communicative standpoint. The objective in this context entails taking the information acquired through scientific endeavors, converting it into a practical concept, and subsequently elucidating that concept to an audience lacking specialized knowledge in the field. The purpose of this section is to explore the process of developing written content tailored to an extensively researched target audience, thereby effectively conveying your knowledge within the realm of their expertise.

And, considering that their area of expertise might significantly differ from yours, it becomes essential to elucidate your message, ensuring they can comprehend and decipher it, before advancing to the subsequent phase.

What is the extent of information that can be conveyed within a concise 15-word sentence, and how many factual details can be effectively transmitted?

Last night, Usain Bolt achieved a new milestone by shattering the existing World Record for the 100 metres, completing the race in an astonishing 09:58 seconds.

There are a total of thirteen words presented here, each of which conveys four distinct pieces of information. The sprinter known as Usain Bolt broke the world record with a remarkable time of 09:58 last evening.

The term "seconds" is superfluous; however, it is necessary to elucidate the context in some manner, as even though one may anticipate understanding, assurance is never absolute. In actuality, the time of the record would be relocated to the second sentence, as it pertains to a supplementary fact rather than the principal one. However, I opted to include it in this context in order to illustrate a particular point. Attempt to condense a multitude of factual information regarding your area of expertise into a concise statement comprising 15 words, ensuring its comprehensibility to individuals lacking specialized knowledge.

To commence, I intend to initiate our endeavor by employing a straightforward writing framework prior to delving into further intricacies. The one we are going to be looking at is the one you see used by newspapers and news media for reporting the news.

A fire ignited yesterday evening on the High Street.

Below, you will find a collection of ten words, each accompanied by three factual pieces of information. This sentence exhibits a more proficient structure, characterized by the incorporation of three concise facts that are meticulously arranged. I have attributed a significance value to each factual piece, subsequently arranging them in a specific sequence.

1, Fire

2, High Street

3, Yesterday

When it comes to significant messages such as this, the utmost significance lies undoubtedly in the fire itself, followed by the aspect of location and lastly, the element of timing (although this order may vary if conveying the event in real-time on a platform like Twitter). What you will observe is that I have organized it in the sequence of 1-3-2.

The rationale behind this lies in the manner in which one assimilates information, in addition to the fact that such an approach is more coherent and facilitates the smooth progression of a news report. The order could be readily rearranged without altering the meaning; however, it is more effective in its current configuration as it pertains to our cognitive processing of information. The coherence of the writing is equally crucial to the architecture and tone, for it seamlessly guides the reader from one narrative segment to another. The trio of facts constitutes the essence of the message, while the manner in which they are conveyed, commonly referred to as the flow, encapsulates the style of the message.

You have also acquired all the necessary knowledge in the initial sentence. If you are inclined towards further comprehension, you may proceed with reading; in the event that you lack genuine interest, you will not pursue it.

However, the crucial matter at hand is that they possess a comprehensive understanding of the pertinent information.

The inverted pyramid is a term used in news writing, and having a grasp of this structure will enhance your writing skills. Thus, let us redirect our attention to the fire that occurred on the high street and resume the continuation of this article.

A fire was ignited yesterday evening in the High Street. The building was evacuated by the fire and rescue service, who reported that there were no injuries sustained by any individuals.

Station Officer John Smith has indicated that initial inquiries suggest that the incident was caused by an electrical fire. Fortunately, the residents were promptly notified by their smoke detector and subsequently contacted the fire service."

The incident occurred at approximately 7:30pm, during which resident Sarah Collins, who works the night shift, was alerted by her smoke alarm.

Sarah stated, "After a brief period of realization that the source of the disturbance emanated from the dwelling directly above mine, I promptly contacted the fire department who advised me to evacuate for precautionary measures."

According to Sarah, it is estimated that the fire service arrived within a period of merely 'five minutes'. They unlawfully gained access to the apartment, and expeditiously extinguished the minor fire.

Station Officer Smith emphasized the significance of smoke detectors, stating, "This incident serves as a clear demonstration of their utmost importance." They possess the ability to safeguard not only one's own life, but also the lives of others and the valuable assets belonging to oneself and others. We kindly request that individuals verify the functionality of the batteries in their smoke detectors."

Therefore, there exists a concise news article comprising 168 words that exemplifies the utilization of the inverted pyramid technique in news journalism. In the beginning, there is an abundance of information, but as the narrative progresses, the discussion of the fire gradually diminishes until only a loosely associated safety message is provided, devoid of any fresh insights.

Given the uncomplicated nature of news writing, I would like you to promptly compose a concise article, potentially even shorter than the aforementioned text.

Compose a brief narrative in this manner detailing the events of your day. Consider how you would articulate it in the framework of the inverted pyramid. What would you consider to be the most crucial component? To what extent can you incorporate multiple facts into a sentence utilizing the previously mentioned 1-3-2 structure?

I would appreciate it if you could minimize the amount of time dedicated to this task, as it is unlikely that you will frequently encounter the need to write in this particular manner. It is imperative to grasp this significant writing style as a means of comprehending a straightforward and commonly employed writing structure that enjoys wide recognition among nearly all individuals.

When I was being trained in this style, I couldn't tell you how many I wrote each week, but it was a lot. The underlying principle is that developing proficiency in a newly adopted writing style necessitates significant and consistent practice. It's why you need to show what you write to someone in your intended audience for the feedback to help you become a better writer. It is imperative that all your actions undergo scrutiny from multiple individuals.

The inverse pyramid exhibits a straightforward framework, and as previously mentioned, it is unlikely to be employed for conveying scientific information. Nonetheless, acquiring comprehension of this pattern will prove beneficial when engaging with journalists who are conveying your research outcomes.

Now, I would like to engage in a discussion regarding the intricacies of feature writing. These are the articles found in print publications such as newspapers and magazines, wherein they offer comprehensive and intricate analyses pertaining to particular subjects. Whether it pertains to a news topic or a piece of general interest, it adheres to a particular format. In the context of news writing, the initial two sentences encompass the entirety of the introduction, body, and conclusion, with the subsequent content serving to provide supplementary information.

Feature writing adheres to a distinct three-part structure, encompassing an introduction, a main body, and a conclusion, deliberately steering clear of the conventional inverted pyramid approach. By employing this particular writing technique, you are consistently presenting fresh information in order to construct a cohesive narrative within your storytelling.

The primary focal points reside at the commencement and conclusion. The introductory section must captivate the reader's curiosity, compelling them to desire further information. When considering the introduction of news articles, the entirety of the key information is presented at once. To extract or elicit the desired characteristic.

An individual occupying a humble position as a clerk in a patent office located in Switzerland revolutionized the global landscape....

What is wrong with your level of energy? According to the findings of Einstein, it has been established that they are essentially identical.

The concept of heredity is evident when observing that offspring often possess similarities to their parents. However, there is a notable exception where an individual made such significant achievements that it contributed to NASA's successful moon landing endeavor.

In this statement, I am providing some preliminary information that alludes to the direction in which I am headed, yet does not reveal any substantial details. We are significantly diverging from the realm of scientific discourse and venturing into the realm of artistic expression, particularly in the initial section of the article.

Communication is a discipline grounded in scientific principles, of which you have been exposed to certain theoretical aspects, while I have barely touched upon the subject. Nonetheless, it is an artful application of these scientific principles. News writing encompasses the dissemination of objective information, meticulously structured to emphasize the significance of facts while assigning distinct weight to each. The mastery of features writing lies in the manner in which one skillfully presents the factual information to readers within the framework of a narrative structure they have constructed.

Feature writing entails a heightened level of artistic mastery. If two journalists are given the same news story, their resulting article will bear a striking resemblance to each other.

If you solicit their assistance in composing a feature article on a particular topic, you will receive as many distinct interpretations as there are journalists. This epitomizes the creative facet of media communications, which necessitates substantial time investment for acquisition through diligent repetition and dedicated practice.

Attending a one-week, one-day, or one-afternoon science communication course would not result in perceptible improvement by the end of the program. Indeed, it is true that you will gain a few ideas; however, your level of expertise in this matter is equivalent to the knowledge I possess regarding black holes. If you believe you are experiencing the Carnoustie Effect.

Carnoustie is a golf course situated in Scotland which served as the venue for the prestigious 1999 Open Golf Championship. The local community engages in consistent daily activities at the site without encountering any issues. However, the victor of the Open performed at a level six strokes above par, demonstrating a proficiency akin to that of a highly skilled non-professional athlete.

The course exhibited strong wind gusts, and the professionals approached it with excessive self-assurance. Jean van de Velde approached the final hole with the requirement of achieving a score two shots above par in order to secure victory. Admittedly, the outcome was unfavorable for him, yet it is important to acknowledge that he was not the sole individual involved. Alternatively, you may consider researching the research conducted by Son and Kornell, which highlights the tendency of individuals who possess expertise in a particular domain to overestimate their aptitude in unrelated areas where they lack specialist knowledge.

The phrase 'Carnoustie Effect' is currently being employed within various fields including the military and stock trading, to depict situations where individuals anticipate a straightforward triumph or success, but ultimately fall short of their expectations.

I also aspire to utilize it in the realm of scientific communication.

This book does not offer a swift solution. It is imperative to engage in repeated practice, experimentation, and acquisition of knowledge pertaining to these techniques.

Anyway, I digress.

After crafting your introductory section with the intention of captivating the reader's attention, what subsequent steps should you take? Having provided the necessary context, you may now commence with your account. Let us revisit the aforementioned example introductions.

A modest clerk employed at a Swiss patent office made a profound impact on the course of history....

What will the focus of this feature be? Am I composing a historical account of Einstein's life, creating a comprehensive profile, or discussing his theories and their transformative impact on the field of science? It could pertain to any of them, possibly even solely focused on patent offices; however, the primary objective lies in fabricating a suggestive element, beckoning the reader to delve further.

The second one follows the same principle.

What is the issue with your energy levels? According to Einstein's proof, these two entities are fundamentally equivalent.

Here, the possibilities are significantly greater in terms of the direction this is heading. Now, we can delve into topics such as the velocity of light, nuclear power, or a multitude of other subjects. It could potentially serve as an exposé shedding light on the utilization of pseudo-science within certain healthcare industries, wherein attempts are made to embellish the purported value of their offerings without justified merit.

The final one is the one I prefer the most. This particular topic appears to possess greater specificity, pertaining either to the concept of gravity or the domain of space exploration.

The adage that "like father, like son" holds true in most cases, but there was one exceptional case where a descendant made a significant impact, even contributing to NASA's successful lunar mission.

The main objective at hand is that the introduction does not pertain directly to the subject matter that you will be addressing; rather, it serves as a preliminary explanation of the topic that you will be discussing.

Now that you have completed this section, it is imperative that you proceed with the arduous task of crafting the narrative of the story. It is challenging to articulate a simple method for composing it. Commence by delving into the conclusion and subsequently expound upon the sequence of events leading up to said conclusion. Maybe you'll start halfway through with the equivalent of the eureka moment of Archimedes running naked down the street. Subsequently, return to the inception and establish the refutation of the crown's composition being gold, followed by an analysis of its contemporary implications.

The crux lies in the fact that it is not necessary to commence from the onset; rather, it must simply be integrated into the narrative you are recounting. In a distant past within a distant galaxy, the cinematic saga began with installments 4, 5, and 6, followed subsequently by episodes 1, 2, and 3, and culminating in episodes 7, Rogue One, 8, Solo, and finally, 9. You have the freedom to commence from any point; however, irrespective of the chosen beginning, it is imperative that the story possesses a point of initiation and a coherent narrative.

Once more, honing one's skills in this area is unattainable without consistent practice. Ultimately, this is the sole means of reaching Carnegie Hall.

The absence of a structure in your feature writing is not the case at all, as there undoubtedly exists one. Remember your introduction? Upon completion of your feature, it is imperative to subsequently revisit it in some manner.

Suppose you have employed the apple and NASA introduction, thereafter expounded upon the theory of gravity through a captivating and enlightening manner, delving into the contributions of Newton, the laws of motion, and the forces of gravitation. One potential conclusion could be formulated as follows...

The impact of Newton's observation regarding the apple has revolutionized our understanding of planetary motion, serving as the basis for predicting the trajectories of the Voyager probes for countless millennia ahead. However, the apple continues to serve a significant purpose in the realm of space exploration, as it remains an essential component of the astronauts' diet aboard the International Space Station, in high demand by the crew members.

I have employed comedic elements; however, one can envisage the approximately 800 words that follow, and how the introduction provided a gateway to the narrative you desired to express. The conclusion encapsulates the entirety of the feature and subsequently reverts to the beginning, establishing a cohesive link to the narrative being conveyed.

I previously perused a feature article pertaining to an individual who had been bestowed with the accolade of being deemed the most erudite individual globally, which served as the origin point for my interest. The passage concluded with the author highlighting their awareness of something that eluded even the most astute individuals - their trousers were left unfastened.

It is now imperative for you to commence the composition of a feature, as it will facilitate your understanding of proper writing techniques. In fact, composing in this manner is quite enjoyable; however, it necessitates a significantly greater investment of time compared to the conventional inverted pyramid approach employed in news writing. A journalist can produce anywhere from ten to twenty news stories within a single day, encompassing thorough research, credible sourcing, and conducting interviews. However, setting a target of one feature article per day, along with a few news articles, is more pragmatic.

In the context of news reporting, while the inverted pyramid structure characterizes the traditional approach, a feature article can be likened to a column, wherein the information is seamlessly presented in a narrative form, allowing for a steady progress.

Please take some time to consider crafting a feature centered around your work or research, and strategize on how you can entice readers to engage with it. If you possess a certain level of courage, you may even endeavor to devise a commendable title, a task considerably more challenging than it may initially appear. However, it is crucial to bear in mind that consistent practice is imperative for skill mastery.

The Study Of Interpersonal Dynamics With The Aim Of Addressing Challenges Encountered In Developing Social Relationships.

The matter of establishing friendships appears to carry little significance for children and adolescents diagnosed with Asperger Syndrome.

However, the truth lies in the fact that these individuals lack sufficient means to effectively engage with others and notably lack the capacity to cultivate environments of trust, thus hindering the establishment of meaningful personal connections and the development of genuine friendships.

This can lead to a level of exasperation and incite feelings of aggression and unease. Efficient guidance must be provided to address and mitigate this internal conflict, ultimately fostering the enhancement of relationships.

As per the Diagnostic and Statistical Manual of Mental Disorders, Fifth Edition (DSM-5), individuals diagnosed with Asperger syndrome exhibit a notable lack of inherent inclination towards voluntarily sharing pleasure, pursuits, and goals with others.

Executing a meticulously coordinated undertaking can facilitate the establishment of environments in which individuals perceive themselves as respected, and where their personal priorities hold equal significance to those of others.

•OCD is Rare

When considering mental illnesses, obsessive-compulsive disorders stand out as highly prevalent among them. In the United States exclusively, a reported prevalence rate indicates that one out of every hundred individuals is afflicted by obsessive-compulsive disorder (OCD), with the severity level being classified as severe in 50% of such cases. In the region of West Africa, over 1 million cases linked to OCD are diagnosed annually. In what manner, then, can it not be deemed a prevailing psychopathological condition? Individuals experiencing Obsessive-Compulsive Disorder (OCD), similar to those with other conditions that are subjected to considerable social stigma, are more inclined to remain silent about their circumstances due to an inherent belief that discussing their condition holds little value or may result in severe societal judgment. In contrast to other medical conditions, Obsessive-Compulsive Disorder (OCD) exhibits a comparatively higher capacity for concealment. However, it exacts a significant toll on the afflicted individual and merely exacerbates the condition. In public, when they assume a facade of not possessing those fixated thoughts, they must exert significantly more effort, when in solitude, to mitigate the distress. A significant number of individuals are commonly referred to as loners or introverts, thereby effectively concealing the underlying issue. Others are perceived as peculiar because, not only do they predominantly associate with themselves, but they also occasionally display compulsive behaviors that go unnoticed by those in their vicinity.

- It is solely inherited within familial lineage or prevalent in dysfunctional family structures.

There exist instances of Obsessive-Compulsive Disorder (OCD) wherein thorough examination uncovers a correlation between the affected individual and one or more relatives diagnosed with OCD or other mental disorders. However, it is important to note that this is not universally applicable to all cases. Frequently, instances are documented wherein no relatives exhibit symptoms of any mental disorder. The occurrence of this disorder is not solely reliant on genetic factors. In most instances, the issue tends to be initiated at a later stage of one's life, often triggered by socially uncomfortable or mortifying circumstances. Those particular moments in their lives are clung to, repeatedly revisited in a fervent quest to discern potential avenues for improvement. It may also be initiated by alternative factors. Therefore, there is not a single underlying factor responsible for Obsessive-Compulsive

Disorder. It may commence during early childhood, as exemplified in children diagnosed with Obsessive-Compulsive Disorder (OCD), and also in advanced stages of life. This misconception has served as a contributory factor to the lack of harmony within numerous families. After an individual with OCD discloses their condition publicly, it is not uncommon for other family members to gradually experience a decrease in their social network or even the disintegration of their marital relationships due to the perception that this disorder is hereditary and the subsequent reluctance to cope with it. Additionally, there exists the fallacious notion that individuals who experience compulsive disorders attribute the underlying cause of their issues to upbringing by inadequate caregivers and an unstable domestic environment. However, it is evident that a significant number of individuals diagnosed with OCD originate from households characterized by contentment and well-being. They are fortunate to have parents who provide unwavering support and have enjoyed idyllic childhoods. It is imperative to explicitly state that while genetics may wield influence in certain scenarios, this is not primarily the prevailing circumstance. There should be no discrimination against any type of mental illness, and individuals should not be abandoned to face medical conditions in isolation.

- OCD is readily apparent. • OCD is readily evident. • OCD is clearly noticeable. • OCD is easily observed.

Individuals diagnosed with Obsessive-Compulsive Disorder tend to exhibit a higher propensity for concealing their compulsive behaviors. Unless one undertakes a deliberate examination, the information may remain perpetually elusive. Seek out recurrent behavioral patterns to alleviate the anxiety caused by persistent intrusive thoughts. They are not quirks. Obsessive-Compulsive Disorder (OCD) is not an ailment that exhibits specificity towards any particular ethnic group, age range, or socioeconomic status. Without proper disclosure or revelation from the individual experiencing it, there is no definitive method to ascertain such information. The mental disorder in question will not be detectable through medical tests conducted at the hospital. While brain scans do indicate increased activity in specific regions of the brain in individuals with OCD, such findings alone cannot serve as conclusive evidence for diagnosing the presence of OCD. Furthermore, Obsessive-Compulsive Disorder (OCD) is not readily apparent as not all compulsions are outwardly observable. Certain compulsions are of a cognitive nature, while others entail rapid movements that do not draw as much attention as, for instance, handwashing or wall tapping.

- Their knowledge is insufficient/limited

Although individuals with Obsessive-Compulsive Disorder (OCD) fall within the realm of mental illnesses due to its impact on the mind, they possess an awareness concerning their compulsive behaviors. This is the reason why the majority of individuals with OCD conceal their condition, leading those who do not have OCD to hastily infer that OCD is an infrequent occurrence. It isn\\\'t. They possess a clear understanding of their actions, the rationale behind them, and the potential impact they may have on the perception of spectators. In addition to their unwelcome and preoccupying thoughts, these individuals experience heightened anxiety which drives their inclination to withdraw from social settings and succumb to their compulsions. Numerous individuals afflicted with compulsive disorders possess the awareness that their thoughts and fears are devoid of rational basis. They comprehend that there is truly no imminent danger and that failure to tap on the table evenly, using all fingers on both hands, will not result in any catastrophic consequences. The recognition of the illogical nature of such behaviors and their apparent lack of control is what renders OCD profoundly distressing and despair-inducing. In contrast to individuals with OCPD (Obsessive Compulsive Personality Disorder), individuals with OCD experience distress caused by their compulsions and seek relief from their obsessions.

- It\\\'s Fun

No enjoyment can be derived from circumstances that restrict one's ability to live in freedom. If it impairs the quality of your life, hindering your optimal functioning, then it cannot be deemed as beneficial or pleasurable. Certain individuals afflicted with this disorder discover efficacious mechanisms for managing it through prescribed treatment modalities, and they vouch to genuinely embrace the structure it imparts upon their daily routines. However, due to the inherent uniqueness of individuals, there is variation in each instance of OCD. This statement effectively illustrates the fact that a particular approach or method might not yield the desired outcomes when implemented in a different context or situation. Moreover, in contrast to perfectionism, certain forms of OCD lack any beneficial aspects. Some of these anxieties encompass aversion to direct eye contact, apprehension towards mortality, trepidation of developing into offenders such as rapists or pedophiles, and various additional concerns. Ideas of this nature have the potential to occupy one's thoughts ceaselessly, rendering the individual incapable of experiencing the joys of a contented existence. Television and other forms of media have contributed to the formation of stereotypes that depict OCD as an endearing and eccentric compulsion. The majority of individuals hold the belief that it primarily involves the act of hand washing or ensuring that the gas is switched on. These findings do not provide a comprehensive indication of the frequency with which this occurs. What is the frequency at which an individual with germaphobic tendencies should engage in handwashing within a span of one hour? Similarly, how frequently do individuals experiencing OCD find their thoughts preoccupied with the fear of a fire engulfing their dwelling, thereby impeding their ability to engage in productive thinking? Furthermore, there is an absence of discussion regarding the family members and loved ones of individuals affected by OCD, who, due to their exhaustion from coping with their irrational fears and compulsive actions, reluctantly detach themselves from these individuals, leaving them to navigate the tumultuous landscape of unwanted and untamed thoughts. Numerous instances exist of individuals with Obsessive-Compulsive Disorder being terminated from their employment due to the hindered ability to make substantial contributions to the organization. Tragically, some individuals even resort to extreme measures, such as ending their own lives, in a desperate bid to liberate themselves from the grip of overwhelming thoughts that have seemingly consumed their consciousness and volition. Some individuals resort to alcohol and illicit substances as a means of temporarily escaping their thoughts or troubles. As a result of their disorder, individuals might exhibit erratic behavior or withdraw socially, manifesting introspective tendencies due to a sense of perceived misunderstanding from others. Rather than perceiving OCD as fashionable and casually making statements like "how OCD is that?", It is imperative that we commence comprehending the anxieties and isolation experienced by these individuals. It is imperative that we gain a comprehensive understanding in order to appropriately offer assistance when it is anticipated.

Failure To Adequately Study Will Result In Your Inability To Successfully Navigate Or Fulfill The Requirements Of This Academic Endeavor.

Indeed, this is the renowned declaration by 'Gandalf' (the widely-known character from 'The Lord of the Rings') emphasizing the necessity of grasping fundamental concepts prior to making any attempt at advancement, let alone achieving mastery.

The fundamental process is quite straightforward in this case:

Have a thorough understanding of your subject matter

It is generally presumed by your audience that as the subject matter expert, your knowledge about the topic exceeds their own, and you are present with the purpose of imparting knowledge and enlightening them about what they have yet to learn. Do not engage in discussing subjects for which you lack the requisite passion and conviction at all costs — as doing so is guaranteed to gravely undermine your self-assurance. There is no greater source of embarrassment than witnessing a speaker who neglects their research and arrives at a presentation ill-equipped, possessing scant knowledge of the subject matter.

Acquire a comprehensive knowledge of the fundamental principles in any given area of expertise prior to presenting; gather intriguing pieces of information, narratives, quotations, and illustrations; attain a high level of proficiency in your chosen subject. As a presenter, employing these measures will assist you in articulating persuasive reasoning through the comprehensive assimilation of pertinent information. When individuals engage in discussing subjects that they possess knowledge and fervor for, it elicits a strong response from others. Individuals rapidly establish a connection with both the speaker and the content, thereby providing an immediate surge in the speaker's confidence.

Rehearse

Even the most acclaimed orator commenced their journey as a novice. What actions did the speaker undertake in order to ascend to the status of an expert? Individuals who are dedicated to excellence do not squander any opportunity to engage in practice. In the event that errors are made or mistakes are committed during the initial endeavors, it is crucial to adopt a favorable perspective, extract lessons from these missteps, and progress forward.

Engage in individual practice sessions initially, either before a mirror or using a personal video camera. Certain experts in public speaking are renowned for practicing their skills by delivering speeches in a vacant room. You have the option of practicing in the presence of a select, trustworthy group of individuals. Any individual has the potential to develop strong speaking skills, as long as they are willing to dedicate effort towards its cultivation.

It is imperative to bear in mind the adage, "practice makes perfect," and consequently, it is crucial not to overlook this fundamental step, as it constitutes the bedrock of achieving proficiency as a public speaker.

Learn

Continual learning is an enduring endeavor. Enhance your self-assurance by learning from the most accomplished individuals. The most adept or proficient public speakers possess the ability to greatly inspire and captivate their audience. To acquire knowledge and

imitate influential public speakers, one should consider engaging with them through various channels such as social media platforms, online platforms, or by attending live gatherings. Take note of their utilization of gestures to accentuate the pivotal aspects, as well as their modulation of voice to sustain your attention towards their communication.
TED.com videos are an excellent means of acquiring knowledge from globally renowned orators.

Chapter 3 Summary

To commence the enhancement of your conversational abilities and simultaneously cultivate a sense of self-assurance, the key point to bear in mind is to:

- Cease engaging in negative thinking and refraining from dwelling on past instances of low self-esteem related to your conversational abilities.

Now is an opportune moment to cultivate a positive mindset and gradually strengthen your self-assurance. Please note that you alone are responsible for initiating this task; no one else can undertake it on your behalf.

- Engage in visualization techniques that involve mentally projecting yourself as a poised and accomplished individual, effortlessly navigating every conversation with proficiency and self-assurance.

- Anticipate and equip yourself with conversational subjects to engage in, as a contingency, in the event unforeseen circumstances arise.

- Prioritize the preparation of small talk sessions whenever feasible. This technique works well with meetings that you already expect to happen, like business meetings and networking sessions.

- Cultivate the habit of enunciating clearly to avoid incoherence.

- Endeavor to minimize distractions. Please refrain from initiating a casual conversation if the current circumstances are unfavorable or disrupted.

- Refrain from interrupting the other party during their speech or discourse. Kindly refrain from speaking until they have concluded their discourse. This is indicative of a skilled communicator who creates an environment where both participants have an equal opportunity to engage in conversation.

• Ensure that you are fully engaged, both in body and mind, when engaging in a conversation with another individual. The nonverbal signals that you exhibit through your body language will indicate to the other individual whether you are preoccupied and not fully engaged in paying attention to them.

• Cultivate the skill of posing appropriate inquiries. It is advisable to refrain from asking questions that elicit one-word responses, as these tend to abruptly halt the flow of conversation. It is recommended to utilize open-ended inquiries, as with continuous practice, one's proficiency in this approach will improve progressively.

- Mastery can only be achieved through persistent practice, as mere knowledge of the skill is insufficient. To attain true mastery of a skill necessitates diligent application and practice of the acquired knowledge.

A Self-Reflection On Being Assertive

Assertiveness is an enduring attribute that remains ingrained within us. It is a characteristic that can be forfeited through introspection. The objective of engaging in self-reflection is to comprehend the extent of assertiveness one can exhibit within a particular situation.

Kindly respond with a affirmative or negative response -

• Do you choose to refrain from causing harm to others, even in moments of anger, considering the potential impact of your actions on their emotional well-being?

• When faced with a genuine need, do you believe that it is inappropriate to burden others by seeking assistance? Do you experience feelings of frustration when an important statement made by you is disregarded?

- Are you experiencing negative emotions when you are indirectly being disregarded?

- In the event that an individual requests a favor from you, but you decline, do you reckon that it might convey the perception that your sentiment towards them has waned?

- Typically, do you assume that a busy individual would potentially take offense if you were to request information from them due to the fact that it may consume their precious time? Do you possess a predisposition for effortless engagement in dialogue with unfamiliar individuals, regardless of the setting or circumstance?

Should you have answered affirmatively to any of the aforementioned questions, it is imperative that you partake in training to cultivate and enhance your assertiveness capabilities.

Smarten Personal Communication Style

Effective communication is a fundamental aspect of an individual's existence. Possessing proficient communication abilities grants access to a plethora of opportunities. Individuals who possess exemplary communication abilities are highly regarded and in high demand. There are numerous scenarios in which it is imperative to have a proficient and capable communicator who can facilitate effective information transfer across various professions, nations, and individual dispositions, among other factors. Therefore, the initial step involves the cultivation of interpersonal communication skills. Cultivating a robust and polished personal communication style will prove advantageous in establishing enduring impressions that can yield favorable outcomes. There are numerous benefits associated with possessing an adept personal communication style. They are noted below:

- An individual's sense of identity is established through social means.

Social factors play a significant role in the establishment of one's individual identity. • The establishment of individual identity is largely influenced by social interactions. • The social sphere plays a crucial role in shaping an individual's identity.

• A comprehensive understanding of effective communication in diverse scenarios, while preserving one's unique identity, is cultivated.

• It is now feasible to articulate your thoughts by means of your individuality.

• It becomes feasible to incorporate your characters within the framework of communication style.

• Enhanced self-consciousness. • Heightened self-perception. • Augmented self-awareness.

• Enhanced cognitive clarity. • Elevated precision in thinking. • Increased lucidity of thoughts. • Augmented cognitive acuity.

In order to fully comprehend the significance of effective communication, one must possess an awareness of the negative consequences or detrimental effects that ineffective communication can yield. Allow us to explore the factors contributing to ineffective communication:

• The presence of apprehension and a lack of self-assurance in regards to your reasoning, idea, cognition, and understanding.

• Insufficient knowledge regarding the circumstances. • Limited understanding regarding the state of affairs. • Inadequate consciousness regarding the matter. This results in erroneously estimated expectations.

• Insufficiency of satisfaction. • Absence of gratification. • Want of contentment. • Deficiency in being content.

• Lack of capacity to adhere to, honor, and fulfill deadlines, objectives, and agreements.

- An underlying incompetence which has not been acknowledged.

Communicate Assertively and Effectively

Effectively conveying the message requires a great deal of effort and intentional deliberation. One must exercise a high level of mindfulness and vigilance when engaging in communication. There are fundamental guidelines that should be observed when conveying a message. Given that the objective is to effectively convey the message while retaining all pertinent information in an exceedingly efficient manner, it becomes imperative to be familiar with these steps.

Understanding the requisite content for conveyance.

All matters of significance and require effective communication should be duly pondered upon with utmost seriousness.

Prior to initiating any form of communication, it is imperative to possess a thorough comprehension of the underlying purpose and necessity behind said communication.

Understand your communicator

The audience holds paramount significance. The manner in which communication must transpire is wholly contingent upon the audience or interlocutor. By familiarizing yourself with your audience, it is imperative to understand how to appropriately communicate with them and determine the level of formality required.

Ascertain the Trustworthy Mode of Communication

Determine the optimal mode of communication to select the chosen communication medium. At times, the utilization of interpersonal meetings, electronic mail correspondence, telephonic dialogues, and the application of mobile technology can assist in the facilitation of efficient communication.

How much to communicate

It is important to maintain awareness of the extent of information disclosed during communication. Excessive and protracted discussions, gatherings, correspondences, and television programs often result in the diminished engagement of the recipient.